Beginners Guide To Forex Trading Bots

A guide to help you get started with Forex trading bots and complete instructions for running your bot in a safe manner

By

Divi.O

Copyright © **Divi.O**

All rights reserved. No part of this publication may be reproduced, distributed, or transmitted in any form or by any means, including photocopying, recording, or other electronic or mechanical methods, without the prior written permission of the publisher, except in the case of brief quotations embodied in critical reviews and certain other noncommercial uses permitted by copyright law.

Forward

This guide is from a collection of docs I wrote to introduce folks to running trading bots on the MT4/5 platform on the Forex market predominantly. Folks would reach out to me for more information on the bots I run and how to do it, thus I wrote the docs to get them fully up to speed quickly but with complete knowledge.

I also support beginners and experienced folks out with a Discord that I run, as by nature there are some questions. By design this is a no nonsense straight to the point guide, about all things bots and Forex needed to get you going with a profitable trading bot.

Using this guide you will be informed about the Forex market, trading bots and how to get them up and running successfully in a safe manner.

The three important parts you need as part of using trading bots:

1. Education - This guide is perfect, it has been battle tested and folks are already successfully using it in my Discord. It covers the majority of what you need to know but you will have little questions and markets are changing that is why #2 is also important.

2. Community - Very important in the early days of running bots as you can ask questions from folks who are already running the same bot. Important in the long term as markets are always changing and nice to compare your bot performance with others.

3. Support - Either by the developer or the community Discord. Not all developers have robust timely support you can rely on.

The Bot Club

The Bot Club is the name of our Discord community where we chat about all things trading bots and support each other in their journey. There is no better source for unbiased information to help you keep up to date and a great tool for beginners to start out on their trading bot journey.

How To Join The Bot Club Discord

Check out either our website or instagram and reach out via Instagram DM and I will share a link to the discord.

www.thebotconcierge.com
https://www.instagram.com/thebotconcierge

This guide is for educational purposes only

U.S. Government Required Disclaimer -
Required Disclaimer - Trading foreign exchange ("forex") on margin carries a high level of risk, and may not be suitable for all investors. The high degree of leverage can work against you as well as for you. Before deciding to invest in forex you should carefully consider your investment objectives, level of experience, and risk appetite. The possibility exists that you could sustain a loss of some or all of your initial investment and therefore you should not invest money that you cannot afford to lose. You should be aware of all the risks associated with forex trading and seek advice from an independent financial advisor if you have any doubts.

The purchase, sale or advice regarding forex can only be performed by persons registered with (unless exempt from registration) (i) the CFTC (futures commission merchants, introducing brokers, commodity trading advisors, commodity pool operators, retail foreign exchange dealers, and licensed associated persons of such entities), and/or (ii) the SEC (broker-dealers and/or investment advisers and their licensed associated persons), and (iii) a state regulator (each, an "Intermediary"). Neither we, nor our affiliates or associated persons involved in the production and maintenance of our products and services or this website, is an Intermediary. All purchasers of products and services referenced on this website are encouraged to consult with an investment professional regarding any trading strategy or a particular trade. We make no representation that you will or are likely to achieve profits or losses similar to those discussed on this website. The past performance of any trading system or methodology is not necessarily indicative of future results.

We emphasize that no information set forth in this book or related website is an invitation to trade any specific investments. Trading requires risking money in pursuit of future gain. That is your decision. Do not risk any money you cannot afford to lose. This website does not take into account your own individual financial and personal circumstances. It is intended for educational purposes only and NOT as individual investment advice. Do not act on this information without advice from your investment professional, who you should expect to determine what is suitable for your particular needs and circumstances. Failure to seek detailed professional, personally-tailored advice prior to making any investment could result in actions contrary to your best interests and loss of capital.

*CFTC RULE 4.41(b)(1)/NFA RULE 2-29 - SIMULATED OR HYPOTHETICAL PERFORMANCE RESULTS HAVE CERTAIN INHERENT LIMITATIONS. UNLIKE THE RESULTS SHOWN IN AN ACTUAL PERFORMANCE RECORD, THESE RESULTS DO NOT REPRESENT ACTUAL TRADING. ALSO, BECAUSE THESE TRADES HAVE NOT ACTUALLY BEEN EXECUTED, THESE RESULTS MAY HAVE UNDER-OR-OVER COMPENSATED FOR THE IMPACT, IF ANY, OF CERTAIN MARKET FACTORS, SUCH

AS LACK OF LIQUIDITY. SIMULATED OR HYPOTHETICAL TRADING PROGRAMS IN GENERAL ARE ALSO SUBJECT TO THE FACT THAT THEY ARE DESIGNED WITH THE BENEFIT OF HINDSIGHT. NO REPRESENTATION IS BEING MADE THAT ANY ACCOUNT WILL OR IS LIKELY TO ACHIEVE PROFIT OR LOSSES SIMILAR TO THOSE BEING SHOWN.

NO REPRESENTATION IS BEING MADE THAT ANY PERSON WILL OR IS LIKELY TO ACHIEVE PROFITS OR LOSSES SIMILAR TO THOSE SHOWN. IN FACT, THERE ARE FREQUENTLY SHARP DIFFERENCES BETWEEN HYPOTHETICAL PERFORMANCE RESULTS AND THE ACTUAL RESULTS SUBSEQUENTLY ACHIEVED BY ANY PARTICULAR TRADING PROGRAM.

IN ADDITION, HYPOTHETICAL TRADING DOES NOT INVOLVE FINANCIAL RISK, AND NO HYPOTHETICAL TRADING RECORD CAN COMPLETELY ACCOUNT FOR THE IMPACT OF FINANCIAL RISK IN ACTUAL TRADING. FOR EXAMPLE, THE ABILITY TO WITHSTAND LOSSES OR TO ADHERE TO A PARTICULAR TRADING PROGRAM IN SPITE OF TRADING LOSSES ARE MATERIAL POINTS WHICH CAN ALSO ADVERSELY AFFECT ACTUAL TRADING RESULTS. THERE ARE NUMEROUS OTHER FACTORS RELATED TO THE MARKETS IN GENERAL OR TO THE IMPLEMENTATION OF ANY SPECIFIC TRADING PROGRAM WHICH CANNOT BE FULLY ACCOUNTED FOR IN THE PREPARATION OF HYPOTHETICAL PERFORMANCE RESULTS AND ALL OF WHICH CAN ADVERSELY AFFECT ACTUAL TRADING RESULTS.

Table of Contents

Chapter 1 - My Beginning 1
    introduce-yourself 1
    My Journey to Date (01.02.24) 1
    Next... 2
    And Now.... 3
    Why Am I Running This Discord You May Ask? 4

Chapter 2 - Risk 5
    start-here-first 5
    Bot Risk, Forex Risk, Margin Call, Broker Risk, Leverage Risk, Martingale...let's talk about it all. 5
    Overall Risk 6
    Broker Risk 6
    Margin Call 7
    Shady Forex Setups 7
    Forex Risk 8
    Leverage Risk 8
    Bot Risk 8
    Martingale Strategy 9
    Let's Go! 9

Chapter 3 – Bots 11
    10 Guidelines Before You Evaluate A Bot 11
    How to Evaluate a Bot 12
    My Approach to Bot Equity Investment 13
    Positioning Your Equity Over Different Bots 14
    Types of Trading Bots and How I Categorize Their Risk 14
    Your Risk Tolerance 15
    Understanding Forex Market Movements 15
    Different Types Of Bots 16
    Major, Minor and Exotic Pairs 19
    The Interesting Psychology Effect Of Bots 19

Chapter 4 - Let's Go! 21
    Ready To Get Started? Order Of Events 21
    Troubleshooting 22

Chapter 5 - Managing Your Bot 23
MT4 - How To Manage Your Bot And My Settings 23
Now For The Most Important Reading On Your MT4 Terminal 24
Drawdown 24
When Do I Need To Panic? 25
Understanding Margin 26
Broker Fees 27
Swap Fees 27

Chapter 6 - Equity Protection 30
Equity Protector Bot 30
Objective 30
Why develop this EA? 31
Notifications 31
Variables (customize via Inputs in the smiley face popup) 31
Triggers (Turn On/Off individually using the true/false) 31
Setup 32
Notes Of Known Issues (Important) 32
How To Setup Email In MT4/MT5 Using Gmail 33
Enable Push Notifications on MT4/MT5 33

Chapter 7- The Long Game 34
My Long Term Game Plan 34
The Long Game 34
Portfolio Approach To Running bots 35
Reserve Funds 35
Which Forex Pairs To Run 36
Account Protection Techniques 36
Known Issues As Your Account Gets Larger 36
My Personal Equity 37

Chapter 8 - Bot Performance 38
My Thoughts On Bot Performance 38

Chapter 9 - Being Successful 39
Important Components You Need To Succeed With Bots 39
Education 39
Community 39

  Equity Protection Bot..39

Chapter 10 - My Thoughts On The Bot Marketplace.. 40

Chapter 1 - My Beginning

introduce-yourself

divi.o \<Admin\> 01/11/2024 3:17 PM
I'll go first. Located in Seattle, moved here in 2022 after 20 years in NYC. Have 2 boys 6yo and 9yo. Been into bots since Q1 2023 with The Fed from Nurp as my first. My day job is a corporate accountant. In the winter I snowboard, in the summer I race jet ski's. I think this is a life changing opportunity for those who take the time to do it properly but not exactly straight forward to 'get into' for the beginner. I dont mind helping folks out and I like paying it forward. Karma is real 😊

My Journey to Date (01.02.24)

I have been into bots since my first one with Nurp LLC, The Fed Bot to be exact since Q1, 2023. The Fed bot works, 10-20% a month on average they claim and I agree that's possible but maybe not sustainable forever, I will share a myfxbook later where you can see for yourself. They have a $12-$20k upfront fee and 1% or so monthly. They have a great community with a spectrum of folks, small account investors to large six figure accounts, along with dedicated support. I would describe Nurp as a 'corporate' type bot company doing a lot of advertising with pushy salespeople and although they have support, they only kind of care..

In Q1 2023 NURP was popping up on my IG a lot. I knew about bots for a long while, the kind of thing Wall St used of course, but really had no idea how to get into them personally, couldn't figure it out in a safe manner, so I purchased The Fed bot from Nurp.

I personally feel after a lot of research since I purchased their bot, they don't add enough value to warrant the $12k purchase. Majority of other successful bots are in the $500-$4000 range lifetime. This can be an inaccessible upfront amount for a lot of folks as it can be hard to come up with the bot purchase amount and then have decent equity to invest, that's why I understand in Reddit when I get comments 'I cannot afford Nurp'.

I track my returns on a weekly basis and soon after installing the bot, I had some good wins, support from the community to guide my way with questions and when the bot went into a drawdown. These returns are awesome I thought, and it is, so I scaled in my equity over five months just to be extra careful. I averaged 15% a month using The Fed bot in 2023.

Overall, between the Nurp bot purchase fee, other bot purchase fees, one account that I blew up (I call it educating myself) I have spent $20k. No joke.

Update 08/2024 - I have been shown the backend code of The Fed Bot by Nurp, and it is basically a license of a $1k bot, yet they are charging $10k or more plus a monthly fee. What I have found after discussing this with a veteran of this industry, is that some of these bot companies are really just marketing companies and here to make a quick buck. Do your due diligence questions, look at the track record of the bot and a lot of other questions if you engage with one of these higher priced companies.

Next...

So then I went on a deep dive into the world of bots, in the beginning via the www.mql5.com/ platform to begin with who are the manufacturers of the software that bots run on top of, then google searches, youtube, and of course then my IG feed was flooded with bot offers claiming even crazier returns.

The bots on MQL5 platform are for the most part scams (along with a lot of the Forex world if you are not careful) but there are bots that work in the marketplace, and bots that are not in there that work great. A lot of developers are frustrated with the marketplace and don't bother listing their bot.

Good developers do exist, but you also need to know how to run the bot which many developers are not teaching at all or do not offer timely support after the purchase, you are often on your own to figure things out. Not only with the bot but for the MT4/5 software itself, piecing things together between the broker, developer and maybe youtube is possible but time consuming. Very few developers are run by professional companies, most are individual developers and not great at after sales service or support.

Bad developers want your bot purchase fee and develop a s**t bot that will destroy your equity in no short order. It will work for a couple of weeks then the market changes and will blow your account. They have Telegram support and pretend to care but they don't. I looked at a lot, and still do, demo tested the more promising ones, purchased some, back tested, and still got burned. Those developers are still around and promising the earth of course.

There is zero correlation between price and performance I found. NURP or the 'corporate' type companies with sales folks is like buying a Rolls Royce when a Toyota will do exactly the same thing. Some folks want a fancy luxury car with all the trimmings and I get that, but for a lot of people a Toyota is sufficient.

But the issue is, it's not easy to find that Toyota bot in the world of Forex bots due to how the whole space operates, and when you have the fancy Rolls Royce being shoved in your face and they serve it up on a silver platter then it can be just easy to go that route.

I do feel that folks are preyed upon by the sales people from these bot companies, very pushy and they gloss over or don't explain the risk in full, and unless you are educated about bot performance (and few folks are since it is very new to them) then you are mostly making a blind decision.

No bot should be purchased just based on performance metrics. Some of the finer, more important points no one is going to show you, like what to watch out for when running a bot, what metrics are important in evaluating a bot and more.

In Q2/3B 2023 I was looking for another bot to diversify since an additional license with NURP would have been very pricey for me, but initially I couldn't find one that worked. So what do I do now....my IG feed was still populated with bot offers, 100% return in 2 weeks (just stay clear of those, they work for 2 weeks then will blow your account on the 3rd, but there are some legit developers, some good youtubers offering good services.

I kept looking, testing, doing demo's, all of which took a lot of time, until I eventually found one that is 1/20 the price of The Fed by NURP, same setup and very similar performance.

Now that I have been running bots for a decent while, I feel the sweet spot for bots that can run for a long time without blowing your account is in the 5-10% average monthly performance range. These bots can run with minimal (note, not none) involvement. Anything more than that range and the risk is too great IMO.

And Now....

This year (2024) in addition to looking for more bots, it is all about doing the right things better and positioning my risk so I cannot be taken out of the game. I have 5 good bots running on real equity, using 2 brokers, 2 VPS and a 3rd VPS running demo bots. I have multiple bots to spread my risk as I have a goal of decent 6 figure equity at the end of 2024, this way I can compound my returns, spreading risk and then at the end of 2024 start taking consistent withdrawals.

I am also trying to find bots that trade different strategies, different timeframes, different sets of Forex pairs etc, and in theory smooth out my return. My ultimate goal is to have 4 or 5 bots trading different strategies, but this may change, I might run more for additional diversification.

Wish me luck. I will share my outcome.

Why Am I Running This Discord You May Ask?

If done correctly, I believe running bots can be a life changing opportunity for folks that take the risk, do it the <u>safe</u> as possible way and don't take unnecessary risk. Sticking to the plan I outline below will greatly increase your odds of success over going it alone. I believe in paying it forward and helping folks out, why not right? Karma is real folks.

I also wanted to find like minded folks who were up for finding and testing bots, as it takes a lot of time and energy to do it properly and I have a day job to manage as well, and maybe a bot that didn't work for me would work for someone else due to their setup. The more folks looking out for new bots, testing a bot on demo and sharing what they find, good and bad, is better than one set of eyes. This way we can all share in the success of being part of the community.

Yes I do get a little bit from the referral links, enough for a good steak dinner, nothing life changing. I'm making good money with the bots, no need to be greedy in my opinion.

Chapter 2 - Risk

start-here-first

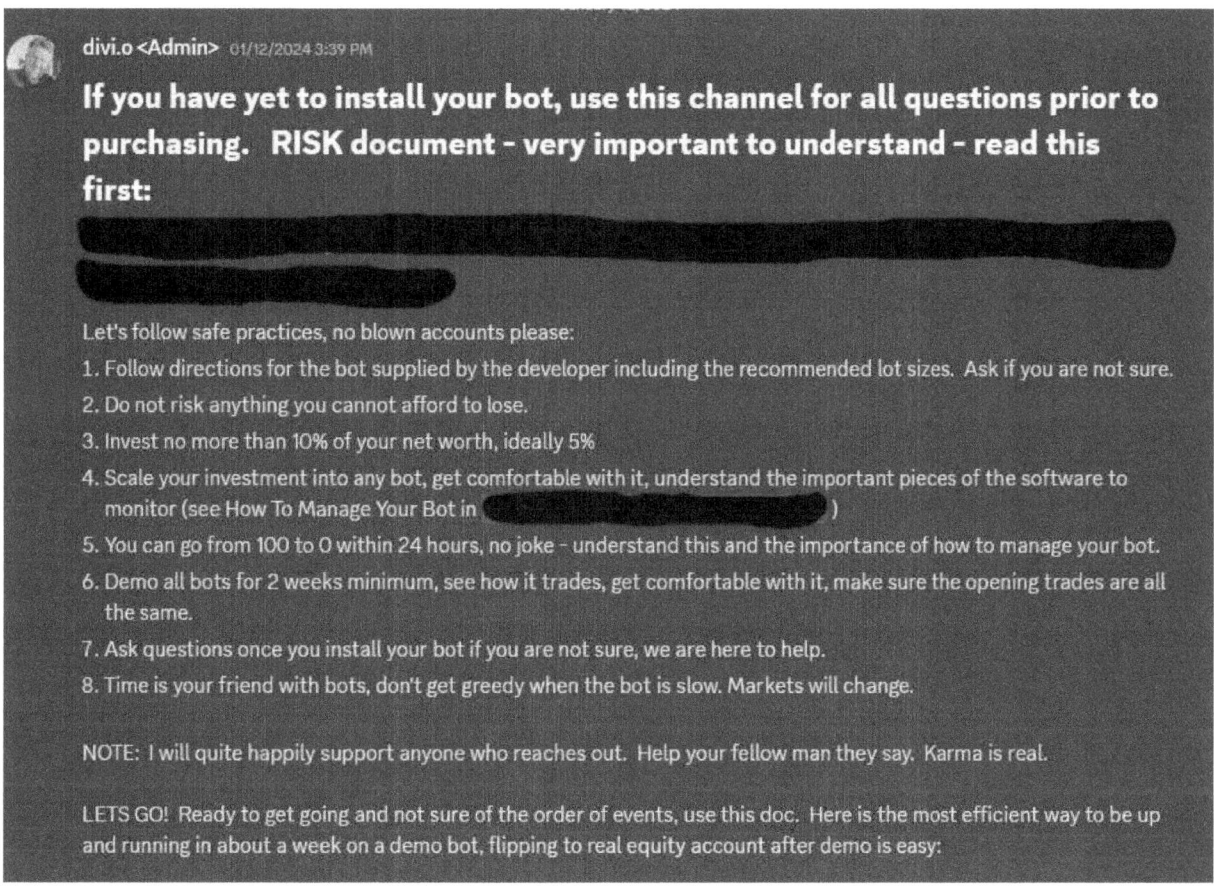

Bot Risk, Forex Risk, Margin Call, Broker Risk, Leverage Risk, Martingale...let's talk about it all.

I write this doc so folks who want to get into bots are fully informed prior to taking the risk. Other than the Bot risk of not working, none of this is obvious for most beginners. The information is from many months of observations and real life experience, I don't mince my words on purpose as this is not for everyone. You are being served up with a direct path to a great bot that will make you money, a methodology that works and I know you are going to think this is easy, but it's not, so I am purposely trying to scare you a little so you play it safe and follow directions.

You can play it safe by:

1. *The correct bot(s) (see recommended bots)*
2. *Proper education (supplied here)*
3. *A support system (this discord)*
4. *A long term strategy as your funds increase (supplied here)*

NOTE: The below applies no matter what trading bot on Forex you use. If it's the one I recommend or others.

Overall Risk

The risk is very real, not just of a 10-20% loss, but of a 100% equity loss with a bot. With the correct bot it will be able to make money in sideways markets and/or trending markets, but managing that risk or drawdown is in my book, the most important factor which is entirely doable if you follow recommendations and don't go adjusting lot sizes, but nothing is ever guaranteed as you are dealing with markets.

When folks deviate from the formula (changing bot settings) without understanding the consequences is when things can go south. It takes time to learn everything, take it slow and ask questions. You will see why below.

There are basically scams or risks at every level of Forex trading, and it takes time to understand these risks and I am working to mitigate that as much as possible on my accounts to make this a long term investment strategy of mine.

It's hard to go back to any of these vendors or anywhere along the line to point fingers if things go south for you. All very much buyer beware. My general rule is to double confirm everyone and everything, just how it has to be I feel. Do not take anyone at their word, do your own due diligence.

Broker Risk

US Citizens are highly regulated, along with a few other countries, because of the danger of leverage or whatever. USA citizens are regulated to 1:50 leverage, most bots need 1:200, some less but there has to be a margin of safety with these things. The developer will let you know what is recommended. Thus, US citizens need to find a broker overseas that will take them on, or use an address outside of the US that is not so regulated (brokers don't send statements out so some are really just looking for an address to cover their butt).

Shady brokers are also out to steal money without you knowing, yes, it happens, hard to prove and keep on top of things, use a <u>regulated</u> broker (I have not seen anything recently like this happen). Shady brokers will close trades without your permission when the market goes crazy, I have heard this happens with the bigger traders as they have bigger lot sizes. To the broker and liquidity provider, they are carrying the risk of you being profitable is the way it works (depends on broker setup). Mine and most likely your lot sizes are very small in the grand scheme of things, this has not happened to me.

Brokers can be regulated by various government entities, and there are of course those brokers that are not regulated. Depending on what country you reside in, very much dictates which brokers you can use. Try to use a regulated broker if possible, but there are also non-regulated but trusted brokers that folks use with no problems. I use both.

Brokers go out of business, it has happened in the past. I haven't seen anything recently though. You need a broker, do your own due diligence.

Margin Call

Understanding where each broker will close your losing trades down for lack of liquidity in your account is key, it's somewhere below 100% free margin as they will freeze additional trades at this point, but before 0% free margin. Each broker does it differently, some will close partial trades, others will close all open trades.

The chances are low of a margin call happening if you follow the guidelines, but this is a part of understanding how to run your bot. A good bot should run in the 2000% plus range or more of margin level most of the time, but going lower intermittently is okay. See what folks say about the broker you choose online if it's not what is recommended by a trusted source.

Low spreads are important, that is their take on each trade. Spreads change during low liquidity as well, during market transitions, holidays.

Shady Forex Setups

Do not use a custodial type arrangement, where you send someone money to manage on your behalf to trade forex (like a hedge fund). We do not do this here, you are 100% in complete control of your funds, the bot, the VPS, everything.

Forex Risk

Retail traders are minnows. The big boys, Wall St, Hedge funds etc are the ones who move the market in addition to news events and trying to shake the retail trades loose. It's estimated that 80% of the forex market is traded by bots. They know this of course and are out there hunting for your bot and liquidity (remember, zero sum game) and along with the brokers, they will take advantage of the volatility to take you out of the game.

One of the better things about forex bots, there is a long history of data to model the bot with. Governments don't want wild long term fluctuations, but in the short term 'Black Swan' events are manufactured by the banks and could take you out, I feel this happens once a year but there are ways to avoid these things, with an equity protector bot that will stop your bot from taking additional trades at X level. Some currency pairs are also more volatile i.e. JPY and CHF.

Leverage Risk

There is great leverage offered up to forex accounts, up to 1:500. Great for returns and a margin of safety, but also means the brokers that offer you an account and will close down your trades in an instant to protect themselves as they are carrying your risk. Understanding this leverage, where to find it on the MT4 terminal and what to do should your bot go down into heavy drawdown is the key to survival during heavy volatility.

I will show you what to do, where to look, this is part of understanding how to run your bot. The chances of your bot getting to that point are low if you run recommended settings.

Bot Risk

This is the most obvious one right. Will my bot work safely without destroying my equity? There are a lot of independent developers with crazy looking websites, that's okay if the bot works. Most bots are no refunds, buyer beware, some will offer trials, a few will give 30 day returns. Many will promise the earth with screenshots (ie Instagram) but no real long term proof (Myfxbook or Fxblue).

Pricing models are all over the map, zero correlation between price and return. Generally they are in the $400-$3000 per year or lifetime, all over the map. Some better ones are in the $3k range but will have performance of 3-5% as they can prove their returns and are a popular bot with many reviews, I get it.

Then there is the 'does this bot with no refunds really going to work questions?'. If I can't see a www.myfxbook.com bot profile (basically a forward test, the gold standard, but can be faked as well FYI) then I'm not really interested or need to do other extra due diligence.

Martingale Strategy

https://www.investopedia.com/terms/m/martingalesystem.asp

'The Fed' bot by NURP uses a martingale strategy, as do many bots. What the bot does is to use increasingly bigger bets for the next trade, for each currency pair when the initial trade goes against it. More volatile pairs use a lower exponent to lower the risk.

Placing progressively larger trades lowers the take profit point as the market will eventually do a mean reversion. What could happen is, if you have say 3 or 4 pairs that go into heavy drawdown (this can happen quickly or slowly) with larger and larger trades placed (this can happen quickly or slowly), that will use up your liquidity.

Not all bots use martingale strategy, but it is effective if you use the right lot sizes as per the developer as these have been back tested and do not get greedy by increasing your starting trades when the market is slow.

Let's Go!

Still ready to go into the world of bots and forex after all of that? The risk is real but manageable if you stay the course and when the market is slow don't start changing the bot settings. Now you know all of that risk, and you can consider yourself fully informed about the risks in the world of forex, take it slow, time is your friend, only risk what you can afford to lose and invest no more than 5% of your net worth.

I run the bots that I recommend, and you can run those bots as well alongside myself and many other folks in the discord. The returns are real and I share my weekly bot returns in discord, along with many others running the same bots.

My goal is 5-10% average monthly return and I consider that risk acceptable (i.e. drawdown is in an acceptable range), while classifying it as a medium risk range considering all bot types. (You can get bots with lower risk and lower return, and you can lower the risk on the recommended bots by lowering lot (trade) size).

The risk is manageable for the long term in terms of bots & forex, which are naturally up there with the highest risk category. But it is up to you to decide how you wish to position your risk so you cannot be taken out of the game.

The pros and those in this game for a long time always take <u>profits off the table at regular intervals</u>. They will withdraw funds so their initial capital is returned, then only playing with house money. I personally have taken out a little for tax purposes at year end, have spread around my funds over different bots and brokers…once I get to $X amount I will take regular profits.

I hope you found this informative and understand the risk of bots and forex. I would rather someone get into bots eyes wide open and respect the risk they are taking, thus I wrote this doc. If it's not for you I understand that. Thank you for reading and I wish you all the best.

Chapter 3 – Bots

10 Guidelines Before You Evaluate A Bot

1. **Is the developer running real equity?** - When a developer runs their own real equity (not demo equity) on the bot, then that is a good sign they have long term faith in the bot.
2. **What kind of support is included?** If there is only a group telegram support it is really not ideal. You need email and/or direct chat support, a community is great but rare.
3. **Does the developer have other bots available?** A good developer will have more than one bot available, a good sign they have used their skill set and know how to apply it in different markets. Note: They could have different performance results which is fine.
4. **How long has the developer been building bots?** The longer the better, showing you they know how to build successful bots. If this is their only bot then you need to look harder at the performance results and other metrics available.
5. **What broker does the developer use?** Is the broker they are using regulated and have a good rating.
6. **Is there a Myfxbook or FXBlue link to the bot?** The gold standard for evaluating the bot performance, you need these otherwise just don't even bother looking further.
7. **Is the only 'proof' of performance a screenshot?** Not to say the screenshot is not real, but they don't give you any information to properly evaluate the bot over all market conditions.
8. **Any third party reviews?** Reviews are always nice if there are any performed by a credible source, read or watch the review to get a better understanding of the bot.
9. **How much real equity is the developer running?** What some developers will do is run $1000 on the bot and see what happens. They are not really risking that much in my book.
10. **How long and consistent are the returns?** There is going to be a natural range of returns for a bot. I don't want to see 40% one month and 5% the next (though if the bot is on a higher time frame, this could be okay). I would rather see a 5%-15% consistent range

over the life of the bot. I like to see 6 months of performance to review so the bot has been through different market conditions.

How to Evaluate a Bot

Here are the qualifying questions on each bot that I need answered.

Please go to www.myfxbook.com and find a bot to follow along. Some developers will expose everything about the bot, others will show only a little.

1. Top left - Want to see Real account, name of broker, leverage
2. Time in service - like to see 6 months or more of history
3. Track Record & Trading Privileges - these should be green and checked off.
4. Monthly return - this is the most accurate on myfxbook imo and tracks my monthly return when I do manually. That large 'Gain' % is calculated incorrectly, not sure why exactly,
5. Drawdown - important. That's the largest drawdown for the life of the bot. But more importantly, go to Chart/Drawdown (tabs along the top), and see the history of drawdown over the life of the bot. Of course the lower the better. Anything below 10% is acceptable with the right leverage, once a month so above 10-20% is okay. Anything above 30% and I want to know why or that it doesn't happen very often. Your account can survive above 30% but of course many factors come into play. Riding too close to the sun IMO above 30%, you don't want to see that all the time.
6. Custom Analysis - click and hit 'all'. Some developers will hide results they don't want you to see with a date range.
7. Growth & Profit curve - generally want to see a nice upward growth and profit graph, dips are okay as long as they are not too big on a % basis.
8. Longs Won/Loss Won - want to see these in the 70-80% combined range. Less is possible for a good bot, but I like above 70%
9. Profit Factor - anything above 1.5 is good, the more the better
10. Standard Deviation - this is a measure of risk. The lower the better.
11. Sharpe Ratio - the higher the better. You can still have a good bot with a low sharpe ratio but it's a good number to look at when evaluating bots.
12. Trading Activity/History - This is left open sometimes by the developer and shows everything including deposits. Want to see consistent gains by the bot, no additional deposits by the developer. Withdrawals are okay of course.
13. Monthly Analytics - look at the month over month returns - This is very accurate. Like to see a consistent return, but there will be a natural range. Click on a month, that will show you what products are being traded.

14. Broker - Should be a more established broker. I have heard via the grapevine that some brokers will offer a developer a fake 'live' account and then they can report this with dummy data. There is really no way to confirm this other than running the bot side by side and looking at the trades your bot takes versus the developer bot.

If all of the above looks good. I will look at purchasing the bot. It needs to fit into my overall bot portfolio now, looking for bots on different timeframes and different products, I figure this will help lower my overall risk and produce more consistent returns as different bots performance varies in the same market conditions.

Once I purchase the bot I will set it up and choose a medium or high risk setting according to the developer, always on a demo account for 2 weeks minimum. I want to see how it trades, the entry points, how often it takes a trade based on price action and especially important, what happens when it loses a trade (even good bots will lose 20-30% of the time) as this is important to understand how it will handle those trades.

Once I get a feel for how it operates, if the performance is good then I will move to a real account, but using a small amount of equity until I get more comfortable with it and look at increasing my equity that I run with that bot

My Approach to Bot Equity Investment

Here I will explain my approach to categorization of bot risk along with an explanation of my overall investment portfolio positioning.

How I think of my equity in bot trading compared to other investment options:

Low Risk Low Return - Savings Accounts, Bonds, CD, Annuities - 3-6% Annual Return
Low Risk High Return - Most likely a scam
High Risk Low Return - Stocks, Indexes, REITS, High Yield Bonds - 8-12% Annual Return

High Risk Highest Return - Forex, Bot Trading - 50-120% Annual Return (Allocated no more than 5% of my investment equity to begin with)

Positioning Your Equity Over Different Bots

What is a risky bot for you may be a low risk bot for someone else, so it is your job to decide which bots to run and the percent equity to run on each bot.

Part of the reason I do it this way, so on a drawdown and if I need extra cash in the higher risk bot, I can transfer funds from the lower risk bot. I recommend 2 VPS if running 3 or more bots, but you will also need to locate your VPS close to your broker server.

1. **Broker #1 & VPS #1**
    a. Low Risk Bot #1 - 25-30% of equity
    b. High Risk Bot #1 - 15-20% of equity

2. **Broker #2 & VPS #2**
    a. Low Risk Bot #2 - 25-30% of equity
    b. High Risk Bot #2 - 15-20% of equity

Overall
    Lower Risk Bots: 50-60% of equity
    Higher Risk Bots: 30-40% of equity

You will need to rebalance funds as they grow in the higher risk bots to the lower risk bots.

Types of Trading Bots and How I Categorize Their Risk

There is no real standard around categorization of bots and their risk, and developers are all over the map in how they define it, so here is what I consider a good methodology:

I generally group bots into three categories, based on the drawdown they exhibit over a long period of time (3 months or more) and what regular Margin Level % range they operate at.

Note: your broker leverage affects the below readings

Low Risk Bot
Generally returns 2-5% a month and does not go above 10% drawdown at all or rarely. These bots like to play in the 2000% plus Margin Level % for most of the time.

Example: Waka Waka Bot https://www.myfxbook.com/members/MischenkoValeria/waka-waka-ea/8379251

Medium Risk Bot

Generally returns 8-15% a month. Drawdown generally no more than 30%, it may go above this range occasionally, once every 1-2 months for 1-3 days waiting for the reversal. A 30% or above drawdown will roughly correspond to below 1000% free margin. These bots regularly operate in the 1000% plus Margin Level %. These types of bots are also good for lowering the risk profile with a lower trade size and thus accept a lower return.

High Risk Bot

Generally returns are 20%+ in a month. These types of bots like sideways markets (grid bots are a good example) but will go into a deep drawdown in a trending market. They like to play in the 300%-800% Margin Level % on a regular basis, and will go below that level in a trending market drawdown.

These types of bots need a lot of handholding and I do not recommend without that oversight and taking regular distributions as part of the strategy. A very risky bot and can destroy your equity in a very short amount of time.

Your Risk Tolerance

I cannot tell from behind a monitor everyone's individual risk profile. After a while I can get a feel for it from your actions, but that doesn't help so much to get you started. I try to explain as best as possible in the Recommended Bots Guide, the risk profile of the bots as they relate to drawdown or unrealized losses.

I find folks react very differently when they see 10% of their funds used up in a drawdown, so that is your job to determine which bots you wish to run and what settings. I try to categorize by the frequency that a bot will visit a certain margin level reading as this is basically all I care about when I am running bots. Your job is to decide which bots fit your lifestyle, goals and risk profile.

Understanding Forex Market Movements

Understanding the two different types of market movements will help you evaluate a potential bot.

Trending Market

A trending market is where the price action moves in one direction with very few pullbacks, this happens approximately 30% of the time. I don't see so many bots designed for this market condition due to the fact it happens a lot less.

Sideways Market

A sideways market is where the price action moves within a range with ups and downs, this happens approximately 70% of the time.

Now if you are a developer, you kind of have to choose one or the other market condition to make your bot profitable. If the bot is designed for a sideways market, it has to have a strategy for dealing with a trending market.

A bot designed for trending markets may place larger bets to make up for the times it isn't making money in a sideways market.

Different Types Of Bots

There are a few different bot strategies that you should be aware of to help you identify how your bot trades. Some developers will not tell you the bot strategy, but in demo mode and watching what the bot does you should be able to identify how it works. Obviously there are many different ways to implement the different strategies.

TP=Take Profit
SL=Stop Loss

Martingale Bots

A true martingale strategy will double the next trade after X move in price action to bring the TP closer to the current price and wait for the reversal. In Forex, the bots usually increase the next trade a say 25% higher than the last trade again and again until the reversal hits. The % factor increase is different for each pair based on back testing and volatility. . There are no SL settings, only TP. This can be effective in a sideways market, and a small amount of trending price action. However, with no SL set, and if the price action goes too far in one direction without a significant reversal, then it will keep placing trades until you run out of margin and then eventually your account will blow.

Grid Bots

These bots love a sideways market. The bot will place two trades, buy and sell at the same price (most likely with only a TP setting, no SL) and whichever way the market trades it will take the win at X but then place another trade in the losing direction to move the TP setting closer to the price action and wait for the reversal to hit TP. These bots will print money in a sideways market, however, unless it has good safety features then you can blow your bot up in a hard trending market. (Advanced technique - if you have a good grid bot and can read charts, folks will look at the general direction of the market and do 'buy only' or 'sell only' trades)

Win or Lose Bots

These bots will place a trade with a TP and a SL. They will not take any additional trades on that Forex pair until the first one closes and usually limit the number of trades for the bot overall. The developer should supply different backtested settings for each pair that is run. They are good for controlling your overall risk due to the win or lose settings. For these types of bots to work for the long term, they need regular updated set files due to changing market conditions. They will usually have a high win rate, but sometimes what the developers do is have a wide SL to achieve this win rate, but when they do lose it can wipe out a significant amount of your gains. There needs to be a balance.

My Process For A Bot To Obtain Official Approved Status

Note: I will run real equity on any bot that is approved, but that equity will be adjusted for how the risk is categorized, higher risk=lower equity. There are no guarantees with any bots from the developer or myself.

It is not easy to find a good bot, it takes time to do forward or live testing to really get a good feel for how a bot works and how I would categorize it's risk and the potential return. Not all developers think the same about risk, some offer different risk settings or guidelines.

After a good time evaluating a bot looking at either a Myfxbook or FxBlue for the most part, once I have purchased the bot this is my process from demo to using real equity to an approved bot by The Bot Club. I take the approved bot status very seriously and I will run any bot that has that seal of approval.

Bot on Demo Account - Approx 2 weeks

1. Set up the bot on a demo account 1:200 leverage, any broker. $5000 or $10000 demo equity. I use the same broker setup for each bot so I have a good baseline to compare. If the

developer gives different risk settings, I will most likely choose the most aggressive one. Will set it up as per the developer recommendations as much as possible.

2. During the testing phase here is what I am looking at:

    a. What is the initial trade size relative to how many pairs it runs and the beginning equity.
    b. How long do trades stay open
    c. How quickly does it scale into additional trades if the price action goes against the initial trade.
    d. What Margin Level % does it generally operate in
    e. Where is the stop loss in relative to the opening trade
    f. Does it wait for a good setup to place a trade
    g. Is the bot profitable? What %
    h. Win/loss ratio
    i. Win $ to Loss $
    j. Would like to see how it handles a drawdown (not always possible)
    k. Timeframe and what pairs the bot trades

Bot on Real Equity - Approx 1-2 Months (Preliminary Status in Discord)

(I know some folks may be keen to run the bot at this status, others may wait until the bot becomes official)

If I like what I see from analysis of the bot while on demo equity, then I will flip to using real equity.

1. The bot will get its own Discord channel 'Bot X - Preliminary'
2. My real equity allocated will be about 5% of my overall bot equity to begin with.
3. Looking at all the items listed in the demo, but really want to see how it handles a drawdown if that happens.
4. Looking at more of the same characteristics of a good bot, but ideally getting a good handle on the bot developer settings and what is the risk profile of them.
5. Ideally I don't want the drawdown going above 30% or Margin Level % below 1000%, okay for a short period. Trying to dial in the risk to reward, that takes time.
6. If there are other folks running the same bot, I like to compare notes on what the bot is doing.

Official Approved Bot (Official Status in Discord)

1. The bot discord channel will be renamed to 'Official' and an announcement will be made.
2. Performance results will be posted weekly along the way and for the overall period of the demo test.
3. I will categorize what I feel is the risk category for the bot (per my risk profiles)

This whole process from evaluation to demo to approved bot takes about 3 months. Just how it has to be.

Major, Minor and Exotic Pairs

I want to mention these as you may see this being referenced, but also in terms of being aware of some of the differences in volatility by category.

There are six major Forex pairs, all involving the USD and these are considered less volatile and generally less manipulated by the market makers.

Minor currency pairs do not involve the USD and are from a smaller country, but generally 1st world. Depending on the pair (looking at JPY or CHF) they can move a lot in one direction before a reversal, usually caused by some news event, the same base currency pair can all go in the same direction at one time and are historically more volatile than the major Forex pairs. But some minor pairs have very low volatility

Exotic Forex pairs generally involve 3rd world countries. Just don't trade these.

The Interesting Psychology Effect Of Bots

It's weird how I have to write this since bots remove so much of the psychology of trading, but they seem to introduce a different set of behaviors to some folks . I have noticed this not just in myself, but also in others so I thought I would write about it.

Unless you have been using bots yourself for a while and found a good profitable bot after many months of trial and error, you have most likely found your way via The Bot Club or another expensive developer providing you a good bot. So you follow directions, install the bot correctly and let it run.

It's making you money, a few % a week, it's awesome right. If you came via the direct path to a profitable bot without any trial and error of a crappy bot, then you may not fully understand the risk of other bots that you may come across.

I want to highlight what you may think is a good idea at the time, but some of the below may happen:

1. You go searching for what other bots are out there and you come across some that you think are great, promising better returns than a few % a week. You purchase, demo it for a couple of weeks, it does great, looks safe to you so you put real equity on it and keep running it. After a few more weeks or even months of good returns, or maybe not even that long, one of the pairs goes deep and you are in heavy drawdown and take a big loss. You wondered what happened. Most likely you were using a grid bot that places buy and sell trades at the same time, great generating returns for a sideways market, but if not designed properly for a trending market then it can be a problem, causing you losses.

2. The returns in The Bot Club bots are slow compared to prior months or the advertised 5-10% a month, so you turn up the beginning lot size on a bot you know is safe and everyone else is using. The profits roll in and everything is fine you think. The next week multiple pairs go on a trend and your bot suffers a big drawdown and you possibly take some losses. A good bot is back tested, forward tested and will handle both sideways and trending markets. Don't mess with the beginning lot sizes without understanding the additional risk you are taking.

Leverage The Bot Club Discord, ask others what they think if you are unsure.

You have an investment type that can produce 5-10% a month return on average, BE HAPPY and SATISFIED with that return, let the bot do its thing and stay in this for the long game folks.

But if you must go out and try a new bot, follow my procedures for testing a new bot (detailed elsewhere) and risk no more than 5% of your bot real equity on a new bot to begin with. Move slowly, give it time to test the bot in all market conditions.

Chapter 4 - Let's Go!

Ready To Get Started? Order Of Events

1. Read the risk doc (chapter 2), maybe twice. I do not mince my words on purpose.
2. Open up a Broker account with the recommended broker, depending on what country you live in. Account opening could take a few hours to a couple of days, depending on support, all brokers are different.
3. Get a VPS, I use the one in the #links-official. Anything will work though but we are trying to minimize latency to your broker. 2ms is what I get but that varies. It should be below 5ms during trading hours.
4. Okay to do a demo on your home computer if you wish. The reason we demo is so you can learn the software and make sure your bot is setup correctly
5. Purchase your bot, see the respective channel and #links-official
6. Get your bot files to your VPS (I email or use google drive)
7. Login to your broker and download the MT4/MT5 software and install (IMPT to download the MT4/MT5 from broker directly)
8. Login to your broker account on the MT4/5 (demo account to begin with please). Easy to change later.
    a. The reason we demo first is so you can learn the software and make sure you have it set up correctly. Your call when you switch to real equity.
    b. Pro Tip: use the same equity in demo account as your planned real equity, 1:200 leverage or higher
9. Set up your bot per instructions from the developer.
    (Each bot is different but usually they are all very similar)
    a. Please ensure the set files are uploaded for each pair, this is important. NOTE: If you are using Ox Sec broker, use Pro account and .PRO currency pairs. ('Right click', 'show all' in the Symbols box, then new chart, use .PRO pairs).
    b. Make sure you have all the chart pairs on recommended time frames
    c. Make sure you have a smiley face on each chart after you drag and drop. (note: if installing over the weekend, it may appear not to be working, wait for the market to open and check on it)
10. Open up a www.myfxbook.com account and link your bot to this. (use the investor password but sometimes you need to use the real password, depends on the broker. Download the app onto your phone (note: updates are delayed sometimes for several hours. Do not rely on this for timely info re drawdowns)

      a. Ox Securities - They have their own phone app, download from their website.
11. Market Open - the charts should be moving and if you have done everything correctly it will start taking a few trades on the first day.
12. Read the doc 'MT4 - How to manage my bot, my settings, emergency procedures', located in the #Leap channel. Understand each setting.
13. The first questions after your bot is installed
    a. Why is there no stop loss? TE bot uses a martingale strategy. Lot sizes are increased if the price action goes against the initial trade, additional larger trades are made to lower the TP and it will wait on the reversal.
    b. Why are all my trades at a loss? A winning trade is mostly quickly realized. Losing trades will hang out until the TP point is reached or the price action goes against it and a larger trade is placed.
14. **Do not** increase your lot sizes because you think the bot is too slow or other. It's the large drawdown you are protecting against.
15. Reach out to Divi.O and purchase The Bot Club Equity Protector bot and install it. TEST the install of the EP bot.
16. Post on discord - 'I am up and running with my new bot' so we can support you and check that your install is correct.

Troubleshooting

1. You drag your bot over to the chart, it appears for a few seconds but then disappears
    a. Check you are logged into your broker account with the correct password (see journal tab)
    b. Should only have one broker account on your MT4 (delete demo account)
    c. Have you registered your broker account on the dev website to your bot license
    d. Check the journal tab for clues
    e. Tools/Options/Experts - have you checked off the correct boxes per instructions

2. You have everything setup etc, but not enough trades are happening
    a. It could be slow time in the market
    b. Ox Securities - you have a PRO account, are you using all .PRO pairs
    c. What is your latency? It should be under 5m/s (bottom right of MT4)

3. Your returns are abnormally higher or lower than the general group
    a. You have not installed the SET files for the bot
    b. Your VPS is not located near the broker server.

Chapter 5 - Managing Your Bot

MT4 - How To Manage Your Bot And My Settings

(IMPT: Your bot is already installed and running on demo, please use this doc so you know how to manage your bot and what to look out for).

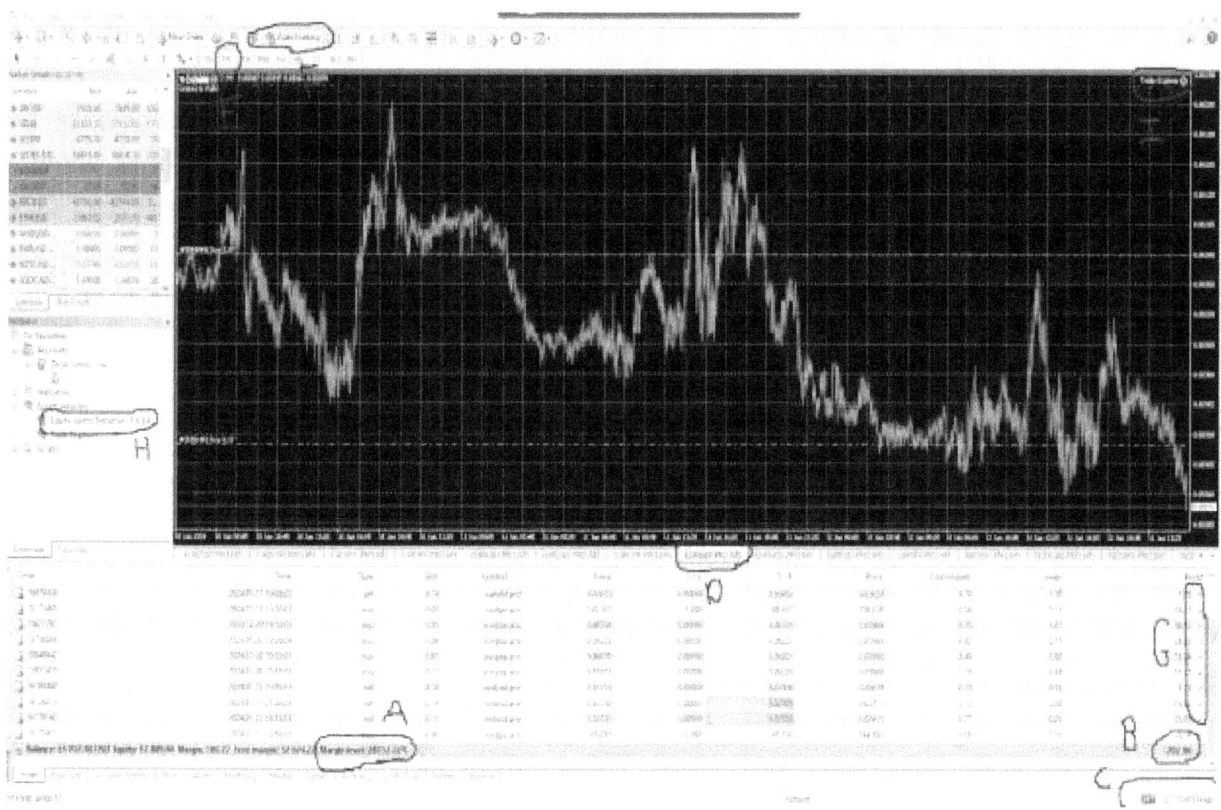

I will go through each letter on the screenshot

C - This indicates if you are connected to your broker. If this number is zero then reconnect by logging in with your broker account details. You may get an 'Update software' message here as well occasionally, restart your bot.

B - This is the amount of your open trades. Another way to confirm if you are connected to your broker correctly as this number will be moving up/down during trading hours.

F - Autotrading button - turn your bot on/off here.

Pro TIP: Everyday I check letters C/B/F and make sure they are doing what they should. Losing connection to your broker happens sometimes.

D - These are your FX pairs and timeframe they are running on.

E - Change the chart to the correct time frame here.

I - Smiley face. This should be smiling (if it's a sad face, then bot is not working). Use this to go into the settings of your bot, and change the lot size should you need too.

G - If you want to close a trade, you can click on these 'X' and it should close with a popup. You can also right click on the open trade bar and the 'Close Order'

H - Equity Sentry has now been replaced by the Equity Protector built by The Bot Club. Lower cost and does exactly what we want it to do.

Now For The Most Important Reading On Your MT4 Terminal

A - Margin Level percent. This shows how much unused margin you have available to you with your broker. Obviously the more the better. Now if the bot goes into heavy drawdown on multiple pairs, placing larger and larger bets as it goes without a reversal in time then your margin will get used up. I watch this like a hawk when it gets lower and determine which pair is causing this by looking at open trades. Now back in Dec when JPY pairs ran deep, this bot handled it okay and went down to 500% margin.

Read the section on understanding margin below. The lower it goes, the slower it gets used up.

PRO TIP: Get yourself a free Tradingview and set up all the FX pairs so you can watch a lot easier what's going on with other indicators. I like to watch at the 1 hour, 2 hour and 4 hour to see if a reversal is on the horizon when a pair goes deep.

Drawdown

Drawdown is another way of saying 'unrealized losses'. Once a bot places a trade and the price goes against the trade, you are in drawdown. Bots will win 70-80% of their trades, but when it doesn't most bots in forex will take another trade to lower the TP, this increases your 'drawdown'. That is the 'B' value on the important parts on your MT4 terminal. (Also see Understanding Margin below as to how dollar values correspond to Margin Level %)

When Do I Need To Panic?

If your margin level is near or below 300% then you can do the below to increase your margin. When the bot goes deep, I find that each extra trade it takes is 100% in margin used. So if you have 3 pairs gone deep, and each one takes a new trade, then that's 300% used up right there.

I do not recommend going below 300% margin level %, <u>especially</u> so if you are heading into a high impact news event (see the Forex Calendar for news events)

<u>Turning your bot off when it reaches below 300-500% is a great idea, thus no more trades can be taken. I will do this and watch the market price, if I feel it's in the reversal stage, then turn the bot back on, but you don't have to for the bot to close out the trades if they have a TP price.</u>

Emergency Procedures

<u>Anything below 150% and you need to take emergency action</u> **ASAP.**

1. Turn your bot off if it is not already. This will stop it taking new trades, and any existing trades will close at the take profit point.
2. Strategically close out some open trades (even at a loss) to restore your margin levels. You could either do it on pairs that have not gone deep, or you could do it on the pairs gone deep and pick the trades kind of in the middle of the run. Obviously the bigger the lot size, the more margin is restored so I tend to do it on the middle lots in the sequence of the pair that has gone deep. You are better off closing out losing trades for a small loss than waiting for the reversal, if your margin level % is below 100%.
3. Turn off any pairs that have not gone deep - Smiley face/Common/Live Trading (unclick Allow Live Trading)
4. Adding more funds if the additional risk is acceptable
5. YOUR BROKER - your broker is not your friend. They are usually taking the opposite side of your trade unless they pass it on. They will CLOSE your trades to protect their business when your margin gets to X% level. Every broker is different and it could be anywhere between 30-70% that they will close your trades WITHOUT asking you first. Some brokers, they don't just close a few, they close them ALL at once, taking your EQUITY TO ZERO

(no joke), others just close out a few, enough to cover your margin. Losing a <u>little equity</u> by closing trades yourself is better than losing 100% of your equity.

Understanding Margin

Let's take a look at a $100k equity account and how margin levels are reflected under different situations:

$99k free margin, $1k used margin, margin level = 10,000%
$95k free margin, $5k used margin, margin level = 2,000%
$90k free margin, $10k used margin, margin level = 1,000%
$80k free margin, $20k used margin, margin level = 500%
$50k free margin, $50k used margin, margin level = 200%
$20k free margin, $80k used margin, margin level = 125%
$0k free margin, $100k used margin, margin level = 100%

A margin level of 100% suggests that the trader's account is at the margin call level. At this point, the broker will not allow more positions to be opened. If the account's equity decreases further, the broker may close out some or all of the trader's positions to prevent further losses. Usually, Forex brokers start liquidating positions at margin level 50% to 30% (depending on which broker)

VPS & MT4 Optimization, Task Manager Readings

After you have installed MT4 and installed your bot, do the below to help minimize your VPS load

VPS
1. Close any web browser
2. Close any other open programs

MT4
1. On the Marketwatch window, right click and 'hide all'. This closes any unused chart symbols
2. Close any unnecessary charts.
3. Tools/Options/Charts - 'Max bars in history' input 5000, 'Max Bars in chart' input 5000
4. Tools/Options/Charts - uncheck 'Enable News' if your EA does not use this function
5. Remove any Expert Advisors that you do not need. Open Data Folder/MQL4/Experts
6. Remove any Indicators that you do not need (Remember TE bot has an indicator in there) Open Data Folder/MQL4/Indicators

Task Manager

You want this reading under 50% during normal times as it will spike when market action heats up.

Broker Fees

Brokers take a fee on every trade that is opened. Usually quote on a round trip basis on 1 lot, and prorated for the trade size. Different accounts within brokers have different fees. I recommend the one with the lowest broker fees and lowest spread. The net gain/loss you will see on your MT4 terminal is after the broker has taken their fee, that is why quite often trades will have a small loss out of the grate.

Swap Fees

(Credit goes to @mike520 who wrote up this article)

The following article was inspired by Discord member Cryptoz and his post. The subject was swap fees which are paid or received on open trades. He included a list of the 23 currency pairs that X bot trades and which side of the trade (long or short) it is most advantageous to be on. He also included instructions on how to find this information yourself.

To do this in MT4/5: click on View and open Market Watch. Then right click on the pair you're interested in and then left click on specifications. Scroll down to 'Swap Long' and 'Swap Short'. A negative number means that's how much (in points or pips) you're paying per day in swap fees for the privilege of keeping a trade open over 24hrs. A positive number means that's how much in swap fees you will receive. I did a little more digging and found out there is a lot more to these swap fees than I first thought. Read on and learn….

I decided to do some more investigating into swap fees. I wanted to know which currency pairs (long or short) had the highest fees so I could block a bot from trading them. So I made a list of each pair and how much the fees were for both long and short positions. When I was done I decided to compare these fees with what other brokers were charging. Wow! Some of them were charging double and some were half the price. Some fees were negative compared to others that were positive. So what I'm saying here is not all brokers charge the same amount for swap fees. Not even close.

It seems that swap fees are a convenient way for some brokers to pay themselves by adding an extra charge called a spread to the fee. These fees can add up fast, especially if you are using a bot that runs a martingale type trading system (like any other bot that gets into lengthy drawdowns). Martingale bots can keep trades open for a long time (like a few weeks or even longer). Swap fees get added/subtracted every day and can make a significant difference in whether the trade ends up being profitable or not. There are no industry wide regulations for swap fees, so these brokers can charge us whatever they want to.

Just in case you are wondering about the idea that you're supposed to make money on swap fees if you're on the positive side of the trade, here are my personal findings. I've been running X bot on Blaze Markets MT4 live for about a month now. Positive swap fees: $4.73, Negative swap fees: $25.05. This is not proof of anything but isn't it odd that the negative fees are 5 times as much as the positive ones. It appears that my broker is getting most of my positive swap fees and padding the negative ones too.

By the way, did you know that Forex trading doesn't stop over the weekend? Neither do the swap fees. So if you hold trades over the weekend you get charged for both days.

The following short explanation of swap fees was borrowed from a longer article found on www.tiomarkets.com:

"Swaps in Forex trading are based on interest rates, and the interest rates are set by the respective central bank for that currency. These interest rates change depending on the central bank's fiscal policy and are subject to change, depending on the economic environment and what their goals are."

"So Forex swap fees are how much you pay in interest to "borrow" currency compared to what you receive in interest when "investing" in another currency. This interest rate differential between assets or currencies determines whether you will pay or receive the Forex swap fee."

As mentioned before, brokers usually add a small charge called a spread to the swap fee rate as well. Forex swap fees are calculated and converted in terms of pips and points." So depending on the size of the trade in pips or points determines the amount of the swap fee.

<u>So what can we, as retail traders do to limit our swap fee costs?</u>

1. Close all trades before 5pm EST (the end of the Forex 24hr day). Unfortunately this is not practical nor recommended if you're running an EA.

2. Swap fees are constantly changing based on the interest rates of the currencies involved. So it's a good idea to check on these fees regularly and if your bot allows it, make changes to your trading system. You may want to turn off the long or short currency pairs with the highest cost, especially if your bot seems to get those pairs into long term trading situations.

3. If you're already in a lengthy trade situation, and the swap fees are growing and getting close to the trade's potential profit, it might be worth it to just close the trade.

4. Find a different broker with lower swap fees. Highly regulated brokers usually have a more transparent fee structure. However, there is always a tradeoff with higher regulations and that usually means reduced freedom for the trader (i.e. lower margin and more control over what you can trade).

Frankly I don't think, as retail traders, there is much we can do about abusive swap fees. Broker's need to make money, and if they are charging lower swap fees, they're probably making it up with higher fees somewhere else. All we can do is limit the damage. And hopefully, now that you now have a little more knowledge about swap fees, you can do just that.

Read the entire article about swap fees at the link below:

https://tiomarkets.com/article/forex-swap-fee-explained

Chapter 6 - Equity Protection

Equity Protector Bot

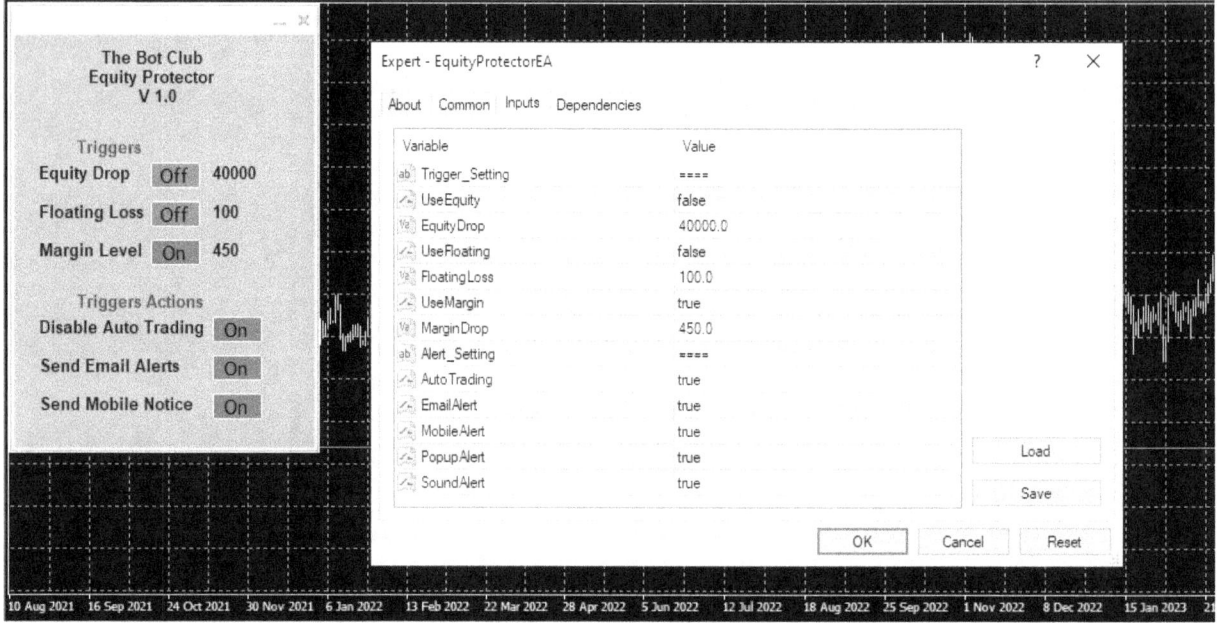

You should consider installing the Equity Protector bot as a very important part of running bots and protecting your equity from black swans or other

Objective

To turn the BOT off when X% Margin Level is reached on the available triggers. It will <u>not</u> close out any trades.

Why develop this EA?

I could not find a bot to just stop trading at X margin level % which is what I care about. There are other bots that will stop AutoTrading and close trades etc, but no other bot will trigger on the margin level %', that is why I had this built.

The general idea is that a bot should have a good overall strategy and you shouldn't need this for 98% of the time, but we are protecting against any serious drawdown issues that may arise and then we can manage the bot manually by waiting for the reversal.

Notifications

MT4 Terminal popup window, MT4 sound, Email if setup, Mobile MT4 alert (still need to confirm this works)
Developer: Divi.O from The Bot Club had developed by 3rd party
Tested: Yes, it works.
Versions: MT4 and MT5
Price: $30 (Paypal/Venmo) each version
How to purchase: reach out to Divi.O in the Discord

Variables (customize via Inputs in the smiley face popup)

1. Equity Drop (Inputs=Use Equity)- This is your Equity value on the Trade window
2. Floating Loss (Inputs=UseFloating)- This is your total current floating profit/loss on the Trade Window, under the Profit column on your Trade window
3. Margin Level (Inputs=Margin Drop)- This is your Margin Level % on your Trade window

Triggers (Turn On/Off individually using the true/false)

1. Disable Auto Trading
2. Send Email Alerts (if Setup via Tools/Options/Email)
3. Send Mobile Notice
4. Popup Alert
5. Sound Alert

Setup

1. Copy EA into your exports - Open Data Folder/MQL4/Experts
2. Navigator window - right click, refresh
3. Open a fresh chart (any pair), put the chart on 1D(just to distinguish from other charts), drop in the bot.
4. Set parameters as needed.
    (I use the Margin Level % as my trigger parameter.)
5. TEST YOUR BOT
    a. **IMPT** - Play with the bot to make sure it will trigger if you set a variable lower/higher than what the current reading is. It should trigger by turning off AutoTrading. This is to make sure it is installed correctly.
    b. It will not trigger if your AutoTrading is OFF
    c. If everything is okay, and it works, make sure your 'AutoTrading' is turned back ON (easy to miss if testing)

Notes Of Known Issues (Important)

1. It may reduce to the below if you navigate to a different pair. Just open it up

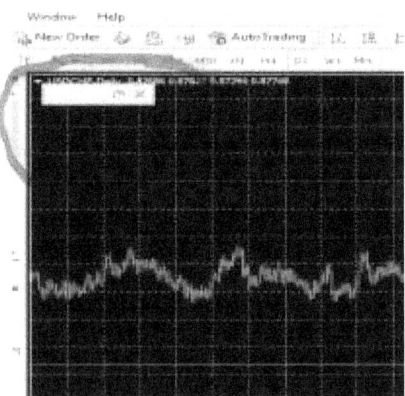

How To Setup Email In MT4/MT5 Using Gmail

https://www.youtube.com/watch?v=Fl8MYrV2bYY

Enable Push Notifications on MT4/MT5

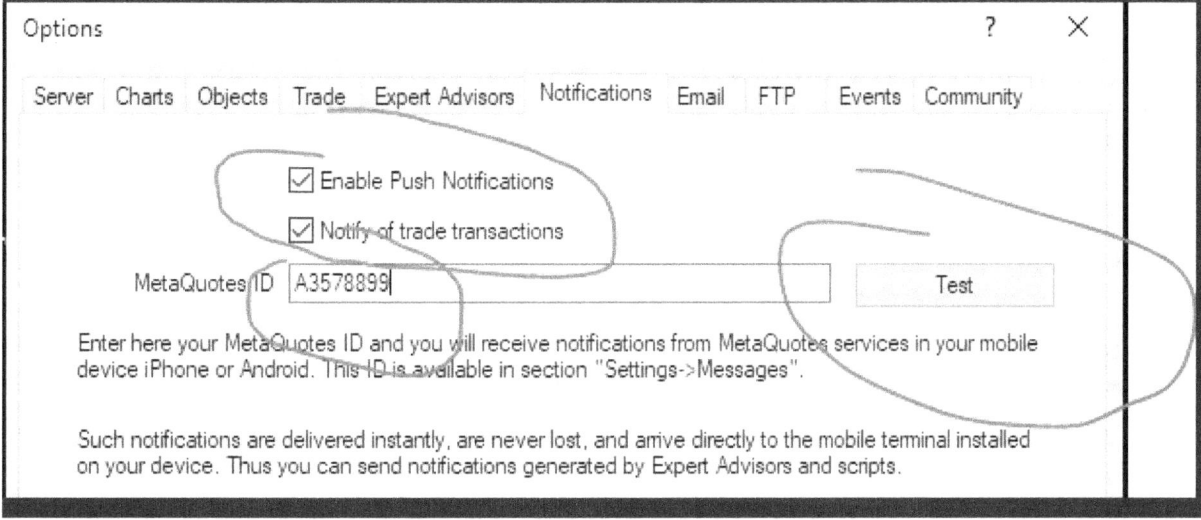

Chapter 7- The Long Game

My Long Term Game Plan

Most of this is included in other docs, but here is a summary of what you should know and then look to be doing.

Checklist - Let's go over what you should know or be doing now that you have had your bot up and running for a month or more. I do or have done all of these things and recommend to others:

1. Demo the bot, learn how to run it
2. Know the important Margin Level % levels.
3. Checking your bot on a daily basis (mobile app is fine)
4. Know how to monitor your bot and when it reaches important levels know what to do
5. Overall, do not invest more than 5% of your net worth into bots.
6. Start first with a small amount of your total planned equity into bots (10-20% of 5%)
7. Understand there will be periods when the market is low volatility and your return could be in the 5-8%/month range and this is okay.
8. Going outside of recommended lot sizes increases your risk. Short term it may work to increase your returns, but long term you could blow your account
9. Use an Equity Protector bot (I know it's a plug for my own bot, but it's well worth the extra safety)

The Long Game

So far I see no reason why forex trading bots would <u>not</u> work for as long as forex can be traded. But we all agree this is risky, and here is what I am doing to mitigate some of that risk and enable myself to be in the game for as long as possible.

Here is my thinking and what I am currently working towards:
1. Multiple bots - This is to help smooth out and help increase my overall return. This also reduces my risk as I can have multiple broker accounts.
2. Multiple Timeframes - On low volatility days, a bot on M1 timeframe will still trade, whereas a bot on a higher timeframe may not.
3. Multiple Products Traded - I am looking for a good gold bot or perhaps a bot that runs specific pairs on a specific market opening hours (ie Japan) for diversity. Maybe a crypto bot as well.

4. How Many bots Should I Run - I am thinking of running 4-5 bots eventually is a good number to manage.
5. Multiple VPS - I don't want a single point of failure running bots, I run 2 VPS with 2 different providers.
6. Multiple Brokers - This is not easy if you are a USA citizen, but do what you can to have multiple brokers. If you are a USA citizen but have overseas relatives with an address you could use, look into that possibility.
7. Report gains to the taxman - All wire transfers over $10k are reported to the IRS. They are watching.
8. Pull out equity - Pay yourself back the original equity invested and just use house funds going forward.
9. Once I get to $XX equity which I plan to stay at and take regular withdrawals, I might turn down the risk of the bots. Since I have a good history with those bots I will know how they run and what % to turn them down and estimated returns.

Currently I run three solid bots with different brokers so I can build a good long term strategy around forex. But I want a couple more that trade differently.

Portfolio Approach To Running bots

The Forex market has been increasingly volatile since 2020 with the changes in fed rates for each country and as the market reacts to this news, there has at times been large trends before a reversal. Due to this, I feel that a 'portfolio' approach to running bots is recommended and should be adjusted according to your risk tolerance. Basically this means running multiple bots and if your bot license allows, running the same bot on different settings.

Reserve Funds

Having funds on hand in your Forex broker account to move to your main bot account incase of a large drawdown is recommended. Or having crypto funds on hand that can be transferred quickly is acceptable. Generally around 20-30% of the equity in your main bot is ideal.

These funds do not need to sit idle, as you can run a bot with low drawdown, get 2-5% return a month kind of thing, and if your main bot goes into drawdown and you need to rescue it, then pause the bot and move the funds over to the bot in drawdown.

Which Forex Pairs To Run

This is really up to the developer to decide which pairs should be run for their bot using through back testing. But I wanted to make a note for you to be aware. Some pairs will trend in one direction more than others, and some pairs are a lot less volatile over the long term, but you do need a certain level of movement to make money. JPY and CHF (but less so) are considered more volatile than other pairs in general, if your bot runs either of these pairs then just be aware.

Account Protection Techniques

How is your equity protected incase of a 'Black Swan' type event? Understanding each of these is a good idea and using some type of protection is a great idea as mentioned earlier. I generally feel that a developer should give guidelines on this type of thing.

If you have a bot and the max drawdown is in the 20% range, then allowing for a limited amount of out of normal activity, then account protection should be in the 30-40% range. Here are some different ways that developers handle account protection.

1. Equity Stop Loss - once your account hits a certain level, then all trades are closed.
2. Pruning - A great strategy as this will close trades in a layered fashion to conserve your equity, you may lose a little equity but not all at once.
3. Stop Loss on Each Trade - Each trade comes with a built in stop loss.
4. Hedging - This means placing a trade in the opposite direction of other trades, this has the effect of <u>increasing</u> your margin level % which is good, but it does use up your equity, needs to be used wisely by the bot, or by manual trades if you can read charts.

Known Issues As Your Account Gets Larger

My understanding is that at around $500k equity on one bot, the trades become slower as the broker/liquidity provider has to find someone for the other side of your trade, whereas with lower trade sizes the broker/liquidity provider may be taking on that risk.

My Personal Equity

To date (07/2024) I have pulled out 100% of my original equity into bots. I did this when I added an additional broker (11/2023) and redistributed funds between two brokers, and also in 06/2024 I pulled out my remaining investment. I plan on adding another broker in the middle of this year (2024) and will see where my equity sits then and make a decision about pulling some equity out and rebalancing again between brokers. I am trying to get to $XX in equity, and then I will pull a regular monthly amount of anything over $XX and put it into a safer investment. Moving funds down the risk profile.

Chapter 8 - Bot Performance

My Thoughts On Bot Performance

How is it possible to achieve these kinds of returns you are wondering?

The forex market runs 24/5 and brokers offer leverage of 1:200, sometimes up to 1:500, and by the bot being an efficient trader winning 70-80% of trades consistently with a good win/loss return ratio, that is basically how.

If you break it down, 100 % a year is 1.92% a week (roughly 7.5 % a month) which is around 0.4% a day, and this is ignoring compounding. This is an achievable amount for a bot that doesn't have any emotions in a normal risk range.

I have run on demo a decent number of bots. It's not easy to find a good bot that does what it claims even after you think you have a good myfxbook that you can analyze. I have seen bots that can do 50-100% in a week on a sideways market and then blow up on a trending market.

You can get bots that return 3-5% a month consistently and will do a very low drawdown of less than 5% a month, and these bots have a good history and cost $2-3k. Looking at you Waka Waka (awesome developer by the way). I may buy her gold bot if I don't find a better alternative, we shall see.

But you need a bot that can manage both sideways and trending markets, otherwise what is the point of using them unless you are going to watch them closely, that is not passive income.

The bots that I prefer that can do this with minimal oversight and with acceptable drawdown, will generally return around 5-10% a month on average over the long term. You may have a few months where you return 5%, and that needs to be fine, as there will be months where you do a 12%, but on average you should get the returns. If a bot promises a return of more than 20% a month, then I start looking at how it does this, and all the statistics to see how risky it is.

Stick to the plan folks, the returns are there, don't get greedy, protect your equity.

Chapter 9 - Being Successful

Important Components You Need To Succeed With Bots

Here are my thoughts on what you need to be successful to run trading bots. In additional to a good bot of course ☐

Education

Some developers will give you good instructions on how to set up a bot, but they do not tell you how to run your MT4/5 and what you need to look out for and all the other little questions you will have. This doc gives you more than enough education to get you up and going safely.

Community

For new folks, there are many little questions as so much of what you are doing is new, very few developer forums exist, the user focused ones are old school with delayed or no response. Comparing performance on a weekly basis as no two bots will do the same thing (even if they are the same bot on the same setup) is nice to ensure you are on the right path. The Bot Club discord is the perfect answer in my humble opinion.

Equity Protection Bot

For the small price of this bot there is no excuse to not have this. Get it and use it. You may not need it if your bot has some kind of protection, but either way, protect your equity.

Chapter 10 - My Thoughts On The Bot Marketplace

This guide mostly goes over bots that work on the MT4/MT5 platform as it has been around the longest. This industry is still in its early days but has gotten a lot more attention in the last 2 years.

The evaluation of bots is still the same though no matter what it runs on and you should be able to look at a potential bot and evaluate it thoroughly after reading this guide

But the market is changing, as I write this I know of one good, but high priced bot company that trades on a USA broker, trading indexes. You can run this bot inside of an IRA which excites me and I signed up for their service.

I am expecting a bot that trades options as well to drop soon, a developer has reached out to me and showed me some solid back tests and gone over the strategy. This will be another exciting development in the bot world as I currently do not know of any other option bot.

Crypto bots are out there if you search for them, there seems to be mixed success with them as it's very hard to program a bot to manage the volatility. Maybe something will pop up down the road.

Well there you have it, the end.

Thank you for reading this far and I wish you happy bot trading!

www.ingramcontent.com/pod-product-compliance
Lightning Source LLC
Chambersburg PA
CBHW062125220526
45471CB00010B/3889